****

Copyright © 2018 Eric Ray

ISBN 978-0-692-17708-2

Library of Congress Control Number: 2018910077

Cover design by Aaron Waters

Printed in the United States

I0158124

Acknowledgments

I wish to thank my daughter, mother, brother, friends, associates, and co-workers who supported me during the hardest times of my life and continue to support me every day. I also want to express my appreciation to the team at UC Berkeley for their dedication to the science of happiness. May those of you who read this gain something helpful that will lead you to a better life.

Table of Contents

Introduction

Confessions from those in my social circle, my own health, the media coverage of suicides, depression on the part of celebrities, and countless internet searches led me to embark on the journey to write this. Over the past two years, I've perused thousands of pages of text, taken college courses, and read countless articles—all on the subjects of neurology, positive psychology, and neuroscientific psychiatry for depression and anxiety. I now have condensed some of this information, together with my own knowledge and experience, here. In this little guide, I present 12 areas that, when practiced, stimulate areas of the brain that produce a mixture of chemicals that enhance our sense of wellbeing and reduce anxiety and depression. I believe we can fight and reduce the effects of depression and anxiety by being aware of, and following Maslow's hierarchy of needs while engaging in activities designed to stimulate certain areas of the brain. It is my opinion that the information included here will help you. There are many factors, including those external, such as the environment, as well as internal, such as genetics, that influence depression, anxiety, and your sense of wellbeing. I couldn't possibly cover all of them here, particularly because I want this to be a quick read that will inspire you to research and learn on your own. Before you begin reading this, there are some things you need to know:

1. If you are having thoughts of suicide, ***seek help immediately.*** We all occupy a space in one living, moving, ever-changing organism called the universe. We are the cells that occupy the body Earth. Therefore, we are here for a reason and regardless of what we are doing at this moment or with our lives, it serves a purpose. Each move

and each decision we make sends a shockwave through the fabric of space and time that creates a ripple effect that could last for hundreds, thousands, or even millions of years. Someone out there needs you, even if you have no family, friends, or anyone to talk to. You can lift up a stranger's life. Go find someone to help. Go find a homeless person and talk to him or her. Go to a retirement home and talk to someone. Just go where other people are and talk to someone.

2. Get a notebook. As you read, take notes on your thoughts and what action items you can do for each part.

3. This is not designed to replace any medical or psychiatric professional, so please continue to see your doctors!

4. I am neither for nor against medication. I believe some people really do need medication and others don't.

5. There are many self-help books, guides, and gurus in the world. I don't claim to be a guru. There is no one-size-fits-all approach to coping with anxiety and depression. However, I truly believe every person can benefit from reading this, even those in excellent health. Consider this complementary to any one of those other books that help people live better lives.

6. This information is comprised of data from scientific research that I gathered from other sources, in addition to my own knowledge, thoughts, and experiences. Each topic has numerous books written about it, and I only summarize them here. I hope that as you learn about each subject, you will be inspired to learn more, just as I did.

7. If you buy this book and don't like it, please give it to someone who could benefit by reading it.

8. I present examples step by step to use all the information here so you can combat depression and anxiety to live a happier and more fulfilling life. Read this entire guidebook first to gain the information so that when you are using these methods and practices, you understand why you're doing them and the way they are helping you.

There you have it. Now you can begin your journey to help your brain work for, rather than against, you.

Part 1: Maslow's Hierarchy of Needs

I am going to explore the hierarchy of needs in more detail here than the other areas because it serves as the foundation on which the entire remainder of the book rests. For example, one of the basic human needs is food. If you are truly starving, you really can't put a lot of thought and effort into attending a social event to benefit a local charity. Make sense?

Abraham Maslow was an American psychologist who established that humans have a hierarchy of needs that must be satisfied. I recommend reading his book *Motivation and Personality*. It is nearly 400 pages long, but definitely is worth it. The following summaries alone will provide you with enough understanding to apply in your own life. According to Maslow, the human needs in order of priority are as follows:

1. **Basic** (physiological): Food, water, shelter, clothing.

2. **Security:** Safety from physical harm, financial security, health and life insurance, job stability, order, law.

3. **Belongingness and love:** Friends, family, lovers, social groups.

4. **Esteem:** Desire for achievement, adequacy, mastery, competence, respect, self-confidence, worth, and feeling necessary and useful to the world.

5. **Self-actualization:** This refers to doing what an individual is suited for best, the realization of one's talents and potential. A writer must write, a musician must compose music. Put others' needs before

yours and act courageously to live life to your fullest potential. This is how one truly can be at peace with oneself.

I assume that most people who read this have met their basic physiological needs, and have food, shelter, water, clothing, and decent health. Assuming these primary needs are met, security is next and it is a major one that changes throughout one's life. Technically, there is no concrete definition of security, as it is subjective and differs for each individual. Further, one part may exist without the other based on each person's internal order of importance. For example, if you have $10 million in the bank, then not having a $10,000 life insurance policy probably won't affect you adversely. In contrast, if you have no money or retirement, then having a life insurance policy to help your family when you die will be more important to you then it is to the person with $10 million in the bank. While there is no need to be paranoid or fearful, it is important to have some level of conscientiousness that this need is being met at different stages in life. At times, you may lose that security and have to rebuild, which is okay. It happens. The need for security can change during different stages in life and if not met, can create problems in other areas of the hierarchy. For example, a single man's security and what that means can change once there are mouths to feed, a mortgage, car payments, etc. He must either raise his level of security or lower his standard of living. Both need to be in harmony. Perhaps a steady paycheck and $5,000 in the bank was this man's true sense of security so he was able to move forward up the hierarchy. However, ten years later, he needs $50,000 in the bank, job security, and life insurance to achieve the same sense of security he once felt. This is his true internal gauge of whether or not he feels secure. Security can be broken down into short- and long-term needs. The way in which, and where, someone grows up can affect what accomplishing one's personal level of security feels like. Growing up in a country where people don't even have their primary basic needs met is different than growing up in Hollywood. A Buddhist monk's definition of security probably differs from that of a retail manager in Kansas City with a wife and kids. Still, both need to meet their sense of security. What humans may perceive as security can change over generations. Now one may feel that a cell phone or a car is necessary to feel a level of security. In fact, in today's world, one could argue that having a car or reliable transportation is now a physiological need. Physiological needs and security needs in today's world are linked closely. Most people couldn't hunt and gather their own food or build a shelter, so a loss of security, particularly financial, could cause a person to lack those. Our ancestors were more concerned about physical safety, and unless you live in a war zone, that probably rings true for you as well. It likely is the issue of security that has caused much of the world's depression and suffering that carries into relationships and esteem. If you lack the basic needs and a sense of security, then it undoubtedly will carry over into other parts of your life. However, just because you have these first two critical components satisfied does not mean you will be happy and healthy. It only means you will be in a position to move forward to address other aspects of your life. There are people in the world who do not have very much, yet they still find happiness and joy. Don't feel bad if you notice, for example, that your sense or need to belong is more important than establishing financial security. Even Maslow indicated that some these needs will not always be in the order of priority he established.

Maslow himself showed best the way these hierarchies play out in real life. Imagine the following scenario in our modern world:

"Let us say that person A has lived for several weeks in a dangerous jungle where he has managed to stay alive by finding occasional food and water. Person B not only stays alive but also has a rifle and a hidden cave with a closable entrance. Person C has all of these and has two more men with him as well. Person D has the food, the gun, the allies, the cave, and in addition, has with him his best-loved friend. Finally, Person E, in the same jungle, has all of these, and in addition is the well-respected leader of his band. For the sake of brevity we may call these men, respectively, the merely surviving, the safe, the belonging, the loved, and the respected" (Maslow 1970).

As you move through each of the following areas, keep these stages of needs in mind. Be honest with yourself. Which stage are you in? Which one needs work? Which ones are you happy with?

Security need: What is one action you need to take to establish a sense of security? What can you do daily? Monthly? Do you need to set aside funds for a rainy day? Purchase life insurance? See the doctor for a physical? Pay your rent or mortgage one month ahead? Start a small business on the side to earn extra money?

Belongingness and love needs: What is one action you need to take to establish a sense of belongingness and love? What can you do daily? Monthly? How is your relationship with your parents or guardians? Your siblings? Can you set aside one day or evening per week to see a friend? What about attending a social event at least once per month? Are the friends in your circle supporting you or are they toxic? Do you ever get together with the neighbors? Can you become involved in a business networking group? How well do you get along with your boss and co-workers? Are you happy and single or do you want a partner? What about going out on a date once per week or once per month?

Esteem needs: What is one action you need to take to establish a sense of esteem? What can you do daily? Monthly? Are you achieving mastery in your work? If not, how can you become an expert in your field? How do you feel about yourself? What do you see when you look in the mirror? Which people on this earth need you and look up to you? All humans, no matter who they are, need to be useful. What is your use in this world? Do you feel important and purposeful? If not, why not? Have you reached any lifelong goals? If you have, reflect on them daily and appreciate what you've accomplished. If not, keep working on your goal(s), because sometimes the journey is more exciting than is the achievement.

Part 2: Sleep

With respect to sleep, you will encounter two types of people most frequently. The first will say things like, "Sleep is for the weak," or "I'll sleep when I'm dead." The second will say they know they need more sleep and love sleeping in on the weekends. Numerous studies have been conducted that demonstrate our species needs rest. We have a rhythm to which our bodies respond, and when that rhythm is disrupted, it can cause a myriad of health and psychological issues. What amount of sleep you need can be determined by genetics and your lifestyle, but most people need between 6 and 9 hours. Please do some research on your own and consult with your doctor. It may take some trial and error before you find what is best for your body. Getting a good night's rest consistently will improve your appearance, lower your blood pressure, help you reduce your appetite and lose weight, improve memory and concentration, and have many more additional benefits.

What can you do to improve your sleep? New pillows? New mattress? New sleeping positions? What about the temperature of your living quarters at night? How late are you using electronic devices? What about shutting off all of your electronic devices 1 hour before bed? Do you have a pet? Does the animal sleep in bed with you or does s/he wake you up constantly throughout the night? If you find yourself waking up constantly needing to go to the bathroom, maybe you should limit your water intake before bed. Don't get me wrong; drinking lots of fluids is always good, but downing a jug of water before bed is probably going to cause you to have to get up throughout the night and thus, will interrupt your sleep pattern. Do your work hours suit your natural sleep rhythm? If not, can you change your hours or perhaps find a new job?

Part 3: Exercise

We all have heard that exercise is good for us. Other than the obvious physical benefits, it also has been shown to reduce stress, lower blood pressure, and promote better sleep, among a suite of other things. In fact, some of the physical benefits play a role in our cognitive health. For example, if you were to lose 50 pounds, not only would it benefit your heart, but your mind would benefit from the stimulation in your brain associated with self-esteem. Anxiety and depression also affect our memories, especially when we are suffering considerable stress. According to a study conducted at the University of British Columbia, exercise that increases your heart rate, such as aerobics or jogging, increases the size of the hippocampus, the area of the brain related to memory. The study also indicated that the amount of time you exercise per week that is necessary for results is 120-150 minutes. In a state of highly active exercise and during the period shortly thereafter, our endorphin levels are up to five times higher than when we are in a state of rest ("What are the Effects of Exercise on the Brain?", 2018). Intense exercise also can release chemicals that cause the euphoric sensation known as "runner's high." By establishing a routine of physical activity, we can begin to reap the rewards of what our ancestors knew all along. Another area you should consider looking into is what foods you are eating, not just to maintain a healthy body weight, but because some of the foods we consume influence our mood positively or negatively.

What do you need to do now to help motivate you to exercise? Or, if you are exercising already, what can you do to take it to the next level so it is more effective? Do you need to meet with a personal trainer? Do you need a workout buddy? Do you need to research online workout programs to try? What about committing to exercising at least three days per week? You can establish a daily plan. For example, you can take 5,000 or 10,000 steps per day. Maybe once a month, you can go to a park and take a hike. Or perhaps once a year, you can take a vacation to a state like Colorado or somewhere that has some mountains, and make it a goal to do a long hike or climb. Always consult with your doctor first to ensure that you are able to work out vigorously.

Part 4: Nature

It appears that in our modern technological world we humans still crave nature. Not only does nature nurture our creativity, it can help us in many other areas as well. According to David Strayer, a cognitive psychologist at the University of Utah, being in natural settings or around nature in general, provides the prefrontal cortex proper time and the ability to rest. He and other researchers suspect that exposure to nature helps regulate not only hormones, respiration, and heart rate, but can calm people and strengthen their ability to focus and perform at a functionally higher capacity than do those who do not get out in nature. When participants in Korean neuroscience research were shown settings in an urban area, the part of their brain that functions in anxiety and fear, the amygdala, demonstrated more blood flow. The opposite effect was demonstrated when participants were shown natural scenes. The areas in the brain that functioned then were those associated with empathy and altruism (Williams, 2016).

What can you do now to get in touch with nature? What about starting out each day finding something in nature to appreciate, whether it's during your commute to work, at school, or just stepping out in your own backyard? It doesn't matter. What if you could just find something natural to appreciate? Whether it's the grass, a flower, or just thinking about the way one little seed is now a full grown tree that you see, and all the biological processes that had to take place to get that little seed to grow into a tree. Think of the aura and the energy that it gives off into the world and the way that tree plays a role in providing the oxygen that you need to breathe. How often are you around animals? Maybe you can visit the zoo? A petting zoo? Or go to a local pet shelter and ask if they need help with the animals while they wait to be adopted. Do you need a pet? Nature is more than just trees and plants; you have to think about the animals, even the insects. Have you ever studied ants as they work around their colony? Have you admired a bee working on a flower? It's amazing. Not only does this get you in touch with nature, but it also causes you to be in awe and appreciate the beauty in the world, which is a topic we will discuss later.

Part 5: Social Connections

Multiple studies have shown that meaningful social relationships, activities, and time spent with others—friends, family, and intimate partners—are all key factors in those who experience greater levels of happiness. This is not surprising. Studies also have demonstrated the opposite for those who are excluded from socializing and are lonely. Their immune systems are weaker, they have trouble sleeping, and the area in the brain associated with pain becomes more active in those who feel lonely and excluded socially (Eisenberger, Lieberman, & Williams, 2003). We have evolved into a social species since we cooperated in hunting and gathering. It is in our DNA to want to connect with others, to cooperate, and when we conflict, we want to reconcile. We want partnerships and monogamy. However, over the past 30 years, there has been talk and research in the social sciences suggesting we have lost some of that highly important sociability. People spend more time watching TV than talking to others. Divorce rates are high. People don't pay attention to their kids. Have you been to a playground recently? Most parents are glued to their phones. Could this have anything to do with depression and anxiety? If these natural needs for social connection are unmet, then that means we lack a key component in happiness. There are three social attachment styles that you can research more on your own: Secure, anxious, and avoidant. The secure sense of attachment is the one in which people are found to be most likely to be happy. Studies have shown that the vagus nerve regulates such things as your vocal projections and facial expressions, is associated with breathing and heart rate, and is involved in regulating the digestive system. It also has been found to be the nerve system related to caring and emotional responses, and has been referred to as the love and caretaking nerve. Studies have demonstrated that the vagus nerve is activated most when we feel a sense of humanity and compassion towards other different groups of people. According to Dr. Dacher Keltner at UC Berkeley, the vagus nerve *"...starts at the top of our spinal cord and runs downward through the neck muscles we use to nod, make eye contact, and speak. It has connections to many key physical functions, including our oxytocin networks, immune response, and inflammation response. It also coordinates the interaction between our breathing and heart rate and controls many digestive processes. Activity in the vagus nerve is related to feelings of connection and care, so it activates in response to emotions— responding strongly to empathy and weakly to emotions like pride. People with lots of vagal activity show more positive emotion, stronger relationships and more social support, and more altruism."* When our body produces a chemical

known as oxytocin, known as the "love hormone,"
we are more trusting and nurturing to others.

Do you cuddle with your lover? How often
do you touch a friend when you are together? A
simple hug, a pat on the back, even a light touch
on the arm, all can elicit your social
connectedness to an individual. When you're out
in public, try to strike up a conversation with a
stranger. This can be truly intimidating at first,
especially if you're dealing with depression and
anxiety. I understand, but I don't suggest
resorting to alcohol or drugs to relax. Take some
deep breaths and convince yourself that you are
confident and that this person's day will be better
if you talk with him or her. Another tool is to ask
yourself what's the worst that could happen by
striking up this conversation? If you can handle
that, then you should have no fear about doing so.
When you are having a conversation with
someone, listen to the person actively and while
you're doing that, take it all in. I promise you'll

feel better when you're done. Try doing this at least once a week, whether it's at the grocery store, your local bar, or a coffee shop—anywhere will work.

Part 6: Being Cooperative

When we don't cooperate with others, our amygdala becomes involved and we feel displeasure. Humans do not like displeasure. Naturally, then, we really do want to cooperate and get along. When we do, we feel a connection to other people. Both embarrassment and apology are emotions and actions involved with being cooperative. Embarrassment shows and signals respect for others. It can lead to acknowledging a mistake and can motivate us to make an apology if one is due. In his explanation of forgiveness, Jack Kornfield said, "...*Forgiveness doesn't mean condoning or forgetting; rather, it involves accepting negative emotions like betrayal, anger, grief, or fear. It doesn't minimize the offense, and we may still resolve to never suffer the same way again. It's something we do for ourselves, so it may not even involve contact with the offender.*

And it's a very profound and challenging process that doesn't happen overnight..."

We are programmed to cooperate. When we were in our infancy as a species, we had to hunt and cooperate to survive. This still applies in today's modern world. What steps can you take to be more cooperative at work? School? With friends? Is there someone who has hurt you in the past whom you can forgive? Is there a coworker with whom you don't get along? What can you do to change that situation so both of you can work together well? Is there a business deal falling apart because two sides can't come together? What solutions can you think of to make it a fair win-win and get the job done? The next time you find yourself in a disagreement, stop and think if it's really worth arguing over or whether you can compromise. Your mind and body will thank you.

Part 7: Compassion and Kindness

Many factors motivate kindness, which is being friendly, generous, and courteous to others. It feels good to be kind to others and it can improve our social status. Compassion is the feeling you get when you see someone suffering and you are motivated, or have an internal urge, to help them. When we witness suffering, the area of the brain responsible for positive emotions, the same area that activates when we see our offspring, also becomes active (Keltner, 2004). Our nervous system becomes calm, our heart rate slows, and this, in turn, helps produce more oxytocin to continue being compassionate and kind. When compassion and kindness are combined, we feel more connected to others by feeling that we are more similar, and the vagus nerve stimulates the reward/pleasure response. When we feel pleasure, it is caused by the brain releasing the neurotransmitter dopamine. Rather than triggering the "fight or flight" response, our brain signals us to want to approach and soothe (Simon-Thomas, n.d.) What can you do to be kinder and more compassionate? A well-known tool to use is to perform random acts of kindness to a stranger. Have you ever been in line at the store and someone didn't have enough to pay? How great would it be if you could pay for that person's purchase? Every time I perform a random act of kindness, I always feel great afterwards, and I promise you will too. A couple of other simple things you can do is hold the door open for people or let someone get over in your lane during rush hour traffic. Not everyone will say thanks or appreciate what you did, but that doesn't matter. That's on them. This is about you. Those simple acts can help you and someone else have a better day.

Part 8: Mindfulness

Mindfulness shapes our brain by increasing gray matter in areas related to attention, learning, self-awareness, self-regulation, empathy, and compassion (Shapiro, 2014). There are many different types of mindfulness techniques, including breathing, sitting, walking meditation, loving-kindness meditation, the body scan, and yoga. Meditation trains the mind to cultivate a certain state, often relaxation. Studies have shown that mindfulness reduces symptoms of distress, anxiety, and depression. When we practice mindfulness, it changes our brains physically over time and makes certain areas respond and connect better, and increase in density. The areas that are improved are those parts of the brain that function in memory, emotion, and reward circuitry. The three primary types of mindfulness meditation are: Sitting meditation, which involves sitting in a relaxed but upright posture and focusing on each breath you take; the body scan, which involves paying attention to each part of your body, from top to bottom, and finally, mindful yoga, the practice of deliberate, intentional focused movement. How can you incorporate mindfulness into your life? Meditate daily? Pray? (if you're religious). What about trying one of the three techniques listed above?

You can find many books and additional resources on meditation. Those below are sufficient to get you started;

- Breathing Meditation
  - Begin by finding a relaxed, comfortable position. You should be seated comfortably on a cushion or in a chair with your back upright. Your hands should be resting comfortably. Pay attention and relax your body and your muscles. Feel the connection with what you're sitting on. Inhale deeply

through your nose, let it fill your
stomach, and exhale slowly through
your mouth. Focus your mind on all of
the actions of just breathing. If and
when your mind wanders,
acknowledge it and refocus on your
breathing. Repeat for at least 5
minutes.

- Body Scan
  - The body scan is performed while
    lying down, sitting, or in any other
    posture. Focus first on the sensations
    of your body. Begin at the top of your
    head and move down to your eyes and
    mouth. Make your way down each
    part of your body all the way to the
    bottoms of your feet. As you do this,
    continue to breathe in deeply through
    your nose, fill your abdomen, and
    exhale slowly through your mouth.
    Repeat for at least 5 minutes.

- Loving-Kindness:
  - This practice derives from a guided meditation created by researcher Emma Seppala, Science Director of Stanford University's Center for Compassion and Altruism Research and Education.

How to receive Loving-Kindness:
With your eyes closed, think of someone close to you living or in the past. Imagine the person standing next to you on your right. Imagine s/he is sending you love, kindness, and wishing for your safety. Now bring to your mind a person who looks up to or admires you. Imagine him or her on your left side. Imagine s/he is sending you love, kindness, and wishing for your safety. You will begin to feel love, warmth, and kindness fill your body. Now picture all of your friends and

everyone who has ever loved you surrounding you on all sides. Everyone is wishing that you have happiness, good health, safety, and wellbeing. Feel all of their love and joy fill your body, heart, and soul.

How to send Loving-Kindness to Loved Ones: Keeping in mind that first person you imagined who was on your right side, begin to imagine you are sending love back to him or her. Remember that just like what they wanted for you, you want for them: Love, safety, and happiness. Repeat the following phrase three times silently:

"May you live with ease, may you be happy, may you be free from pain."

Now bring your focus and awareness to

that same person who was on your left side. Send all of your love and warmth his or her way. Remember that just like what she or he wanted for you, you want for him or her: Love, safety, and happiness. You both want a good life. Repeat the following phrase three times silently:

"Just as I wish to, may you be safe, may you be healthy, may you live with ease and happiness."

Now think of another person you love, friend or family, for example, and send love and warmth his or her way. Repeat the following phrase three times silently:

"May your life be filled with happiness, health, and well-being."

How to send Loving-Kindness to Neutral People: Now think of an acquaintance, co-worker, or someone you don't know very well and toward whom you do not have any particular feeling. You both wish to have a good life. Send all your wishes for love, warmth, security, and well-being to that person. Repeat the following phrase three times silently:

"Just as I wish to, may you also live with ease and happiness. May you be happy, may you be healthy, may you be free from all pain."

How to send Loving-Kindness to All Living Beings: Now expand your awareness and picture the Earth and the entire universe, galaxies, and stars. Bring your focus and awareness to all

living beings whom you can imagine.
Send all of your love and warmth their
way. Repeat the following phrase three
times silently:

*"Just as I wish to, may you live with ease,
happiness, and good health."*

Continue to inhale deeply and exhale.
Notice the way you feel and reflect for a
few moments. When you're done, you can
open your eyes and get up slowly.
Stretch. You'll feel much better.

Part 9: Self Love & Self-Compassion

Self-compassion is a concept Kristin Neff developed, which means changing our inner dialogue from critical to supportive, understanding, and caring. The three steps to self-compassion are: Self-kindness, when we comfort ourselves to alleviate as much stress and emotional pain as possible. Second is having the feeling of community with all humans, knowing we all have similar problems. Last is just being mindful and able to take in our suffering and accept it, deal with it, and move on. There is another state of being when a person is in their "flow." That's when one is engaged in an activity with such focused and passionate intensity that everything else takes second priority. Daniel Goleman stated that for flow to occur, *"...we need to have a clear goal and our skills need to match the challenge in front of us. We also need an environment where we can fully concentrate, and immediate feedback on whether we're moving in the right direction."*

What is your passion? What gets you so engrossed in the activity that you lose track of time? If you don't know, no need to panic. There are plenty of articles and books online or in the library that can help you. A quick search will give you a plethora of options. What can you do every day? Look at yourself in the mirror and repeat how you love yourself and how much you are needed and loved in this world. Look at any flaws you have and focus on understanding them and accepting them for what they are, if you are unable to change them. If you can change and want to change them, appreciate it and think about how you will do so. What steps or actions do you need to take? Further, forgive yourself for any wrongs you may have done. Don't forget about them, but forgive yourself and move on.

Part 10: Gratitude

The two types of gratitude are momentary and long term. In momentary gratitude, we sense and experience the feeling when someone does something for us that benefits us in some way. Long term is when we make habits that promote an enduring sense that, in itself, life is a gift (Emmons, 2010). We begin to see that everything happens for a reason and whether it is challenging or pleasurable, we learn valuable lessons and perceive it optimistically. Gratitude provides physiological and psychological benefits. We can reduce depression and anxiety, increase energy, lower blood pressure, sleep better, be more alert, have less chronic pain, and a sense of attraction to others overall. When we are happy, joyful, and grateful, the aura we give off attracts others into our lives. Now, being grateful doesn't mean we are excited about everything that happens. No one is going to be grateful about getting a flat tire on the way to work during rush hour traffic. However, grateful people will be able to handle that experience better than will those who view the world with skepticism and pessimism. Most habits take constant time and attention to develop, and gratitude is no exception. Being too busy can lead to reduced happiness because gratitude requires time for reflection. We are organisms that strive to achieve goals and function best when we have a goal or goals. Regardless of how small they are, goals help us. Thus, as we achieve more goals, no matter how small, we can reflect and be thankful for the opportunity even to have them and the ability to achieve them. Can you start a gratitude journal? Write in it daily and appreciate everything you have. Who has done something kind for you lately? Write that person a thank you card or letter. Take a moment to imagine yourself without the people and possessions in your life about which you care. Once you feel the

45

pain from this, then you will appreciate and be more grateful for those people and possessions.

Part 11: Being in Awe

Being in awe and admiring beauty, whether man made or natural, can enhance happiness. Whether we are looking out over the vast Grand Canyon, driving down the iconic Las Vegas strip, or looking at pictures of space, it awakens our senses that give us a deeper sense of meaning and appreciation. It makes us realize how vast our universe is and how small a part we play in it. Yasmin Anwar wrote in her article, "Can Awe Boost Health" that experiencing more positive emotions on a given day—particularly awe, wonder, and amazement—are associated with lower levels of the cytokine Interleukin 6, a marker of inflammation. Elevated levels of cytokines are associated with poorer health, including Type 2 diabetes, heart disease, arthritis, Alzheimer's, and clinical depression. What can you do to be in awe? Go on vacation somewhere exotic. Enjoy the morning sunrise.

Watch the snow fall and marvel at the fact that each individual snowflake is unique. Watch a science documentary. Look at the moon and stars one night and imagine all the possibilities in the universe.

Part 12: Volunteerism

Helping others is beneficial not only to the general welfare of those on the receiving end, but it provides us with many benefits as well. Some of these include connecting you to other people, expanding your social connections, and bringing meaning and fulfillment to your life. Moreover, those connections and experiences could help advance your career. According to Helpguide.org, volunteering can improve our health, especially depression and anxiety. It can lower blood pressure, boost confidence and self-esteem, release the hormones and chemicals in our bodies related to wellbeing, and improve cognition. Many places are looking for volunteers constantly. You can search online, but you probably already know of a nonprofit or local religious organization that could use your help. Can you spare time weekly or monthly to

volunteer and help others? It will provide a
lifetime of benefits to your health and happiness.

Final Thoughts

You have now read through the 12 ways to help you combat depression and anxiety and live a better life. Now it's time to put them to use. The following steps will lay the groundwork for you to begin acting upon these activities and developing them into habits. Ultimately, they will become your natural lifestyle. You will have to determine the particular activities that suit you best. It is important that you spend some time keeping each of these topics at the top of your mind. By being mindful and aware of each of these, thoughts will translate into actions, and those actions into habits. To stay on track, I suggest setting an alarm in your phone or putting reminders on your calendar. Get into the habit of reading your personal guide daily as well. Dr. Emiliana Simon-Thomas at the Greater Good Science Center at the UC Berkeley says that the activities that make one person happy will likely be different from those of another. She states that there are six factors that play a role:

1. Motivation and effort: How driven and committed we are to doing something.
2. Efficacy beliefs: Whether we believe we can do it and that it will work.
3. Baseline affective state: How happy we are naturally.
4. Social support: Whether other people will encourage us to do it.
5. Demographics: Age, sex, culture, socioeconomic status.
6. Characteristics of the activity: How often, how much, and what type of activity it is.

One last thought that doesn't have to do with the topics discussed, but will improve our lives and that of everyone with whom we cross paths is work and people of different social classes. One thing we must understand is that we all should strive to be more compassionate and empathetic. The poor person who says millionaires are greedy and all they care about is money has no idea how hard those people may have had to work, the risks they took, and the time lost with friends and family, to create a product or service for others. Moreover, other people are likely to have jobs because of that person; thus, the 97% of us who have jobs wouldn't have them without others' efforts and sacrifices. On the other hand, millionaires and those well off shouldn't look down on the poor and homeless. Everyone has a story, but not everyone's story is the same. Just because you overcame some problem doesn't mean everyone else can. If you are successful, help your fellow people and treat them with dignity and respect. Further, without those who are the working poor, businesses would fail and those higher up the corporate chain wouldn't have jobs. It goes both ways. If you can look at your work and people from this perspective, I promise you will have a better life.

STEPS IN ACTION

1. Get the proper amount of sleep (research and consult your doctor)
2. Exercise (research and consult your doctor)
3. Get out in Nature
4. Establish your subjective sense of security
5. Engage in meaningful social relationships and connections
6. Be cooperative
7. Show compassion & kindness
8. Be mindful and meditate
9. Practice self-compassion
10. Be grateful
11. Be in awe, appreciate beauty and wonder
12. Volunteer
13. Develop your self-esteem

References

Eisenberger, N., Lieberman, M., & Williams, K. (2003). *Science Magazine* (302).

Emmons, R. (2010). Why Gratitude Is Good. Retrieved from https://greatergood.berkeley.edu/article/item /why_gratitude_is_good

Keltner, D. (2004). The Compassionate Instinct. Retrieved from https://greatergood.berkeley.edu/article/item /the_compassionate_instinct

Maslow, A. (1970). *Motivation and Personality*. New York, NY: Harper & Row Publishers, Inc.

Shapiro, S. (2014). How Meditation Changes the Brain. Retrieved from

https://greatergood.berkeley.edu/video/item/
mindfulness_meditation_and_the_brain

Simon-Thomas, E. What's Good About
Compassion? *The Greater Good*. Retrieved
from https://greatergood.berkeley.edu/

What Are the Effects of Exercise on the Brain?
(2018). Retrieved from
https://shop.vescape.com/en/blog/9_what-
are-the-effects-of-exercise-on-the-brain.html

Williams, F. (2016). This Is Your Brain on
Nature. Retrieved from
https://www.nationalgeographic.com/magazi
ne/2016/01/call-to-wild/

www.ingramcontent.com/pod-product-compliance
Lightning Source LLC
Chambersburg PA
CBHW060616030426
42337CB00018B/3074